Gardening

Indoor Gardens

Lori Kinstad Pupeza

ABDO Publishing Company

visit us at
www.abdopub.com

Published by ABDO Publishing Company, 4940 Viking Drive, Edina, Minnesota 55435.
Copyright © 2002 by Abdo Consulting Group, Inc. International copyrights reserved in
all countries. No part of this book may be reproduced in any form without written
permission from the publisher.
Printed in the United States.

Photo credits: Corbis
Contributing editors: Bob Italia, Tamara L. Britton, Kate A. Furlong, Kristin Van Cleaf
Book design and graphics: Neil Klinepier

Library of Congress Cataloging-in-Publication Data

Pupeza, Lori Kinstad.
    Indoor gardens / Lori Kinstad Pupeza.
       p.   cm. -- (Gardening)
    Includes index.
    Summary: Describes how to plan and create an indoor garden,
discussing propagation, making a terrarium, potting plants, feeding
and watering, pests, and other problems.
    ISBN 1-57765-035-2
    1. Indoor gardening--Juvenile literature. [1. Indoor gardening.
2. Gardening.] I. Title. II. Series: Pupeza, Lori Kinstead.
Gardening.
SB419.2.P87 2002
635.9'65--dc21
                          98-029325

Dial Before You Dig

Before digging in your yard with a motorized tiller, call your local utility
company to determine the location of underground utility lines.

Contents

Indoor Gardens 4

Making Plans 6

Gathering Supplies... 8

Planting Seeds 10

Planting Seedlings 12

Propagation.. 14

The Right Spot... 16

Terrariums 18

Greenhouses 20

Caring for Your Garden 22

Pests & Problems 24

An Indoor Project.. 26

Indoor Plants to Try..................................... 28

Glossary... 30

Web Sites 31

Index 32

Indoor Gardens

If you have a small yard or live in an apartment, indoor gardening is perfect for you! Everything plants need to grow can be provided for them indoors. Growing plants indoors will show you firsthand the wonders of nature.

There are many kinds of indoor gardens. You can fill a sunny windowsill with houseplants. You can create a **miniature** landscape in a terrarium. Or you can grow plants in a greenhouse.

To begin your indoor garden, you will need to start planning. First decide what kinds of plants you like and determine where they will grow well. Then it's time to gather your supplies and begin planting. Soon, your garden will be growing!

Planting and caring for an indoor garden can be fun!

Making Plans

Making a plan is important for a successful indoor garden. What kinds of plants do you want to grow? A small, green ivy? A big, leafy palm tree? A prickly cactus? A meat-eating Venus's-flytrap?

Look at books or magazines about plants and terrariums, and see what you like. Go to a garden center and look at all the different plants.

As you plan your garden, you may want to keep a journal. It is a good place to keep notes on the plants you plan to grow in your garden.

Later, you can use your journal to keep a daily record. You can record how you cared for your garden and when your plants bloomed. This will show you how your plants have grown and changed over time.

Would you like to grow a Venus's-flytrap in your garden? It traps insects in its pads, which close up and smother the insect. It takes the plant between 5 and 10 days to digest an insect.

Gathering Supplies

Before you start your indoor garden, it is a good idea to gather all of your supplies together. You will need **seedlings** or seeds, containers, potting soil, **fertilizer**, and a watering can.

If you just want to grow houseplants, you can use any kind of pots. Plants aren't picky about what kind of containers they grow in, so be creative!

If you build a terrarium, you will need a glass container. Some gardeners like to use empty fish tanks. They are big enough to hold many plants.

Determine which type of soil your plants grow best in. Most plants grow well in soft, black soil. Other plants grow best in rocks, wood chips, or sand. It's a good idea to add a little fertilizer to the soil you've chosen.

A watering can is a useful tool for an indoor garden. Watering cans make it easy to control where you are putting the water.

Gardening Tools

Turning Soil & Weeding

Hoe

Raking

Garden Rake

Watering

Watering Can

Hose

Planting

Trowel

Digging

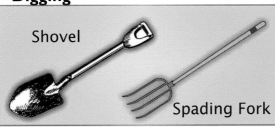

Shovel

Spading Fork

Pest Control

Sprayer

Planting Seeds

Once you've gathered your supplies, it's time to begin planting. One way to start an indoor garden is to plant seeds. Two good plants to grow from seed are cosmoses and marigolds. With a lot of sun and water, they will bloom for several months.

To plant your seeds, you will need containers, seeds, potting soil, and gravel. Place the gravel in the bottom of the pot and fill the container with potting soil. Next, plant the seeds and cover them with a thin layer of soil. Water them until the soil is evenly moist.

Soon, your seeds will **germinate**. Little green shoots called **seedlings** will start to appear in the soil. The seedling's stems and roots will quickly become bigger. Then, buds will form and open into beautiful flowers!

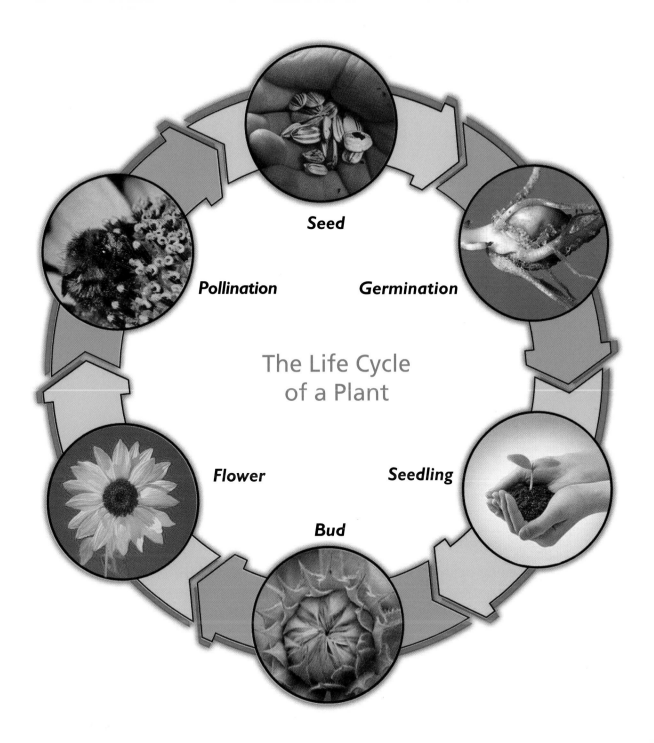

Seed

Germination

Pollination

The Life Cycle
of a Plant

Flower

Seedling

Bud

Planting Seedlings

Another way to start an indoor garden is by planting **seedlings**. Make sure that the pot you use is clean and free of old dirt. Fill the bottom of the pot with rocks or gravel for **drainage**. Then fill it with potting soil.

Potting soil is made up of soil, perlite, and **peat moss**. Soil gives the plants **nutrients** to grow well. Perlite is little white balls that help the soil to drain excess water. Peat moss prevents the soil from drying out completely.

Once you've filled your container with potting soil, it's time to plant! Pick up the container holding the seedling. Turn the container upside down. Hold onto the seedling and gently pull it out of the container. Be careful to not damage the plant.

Once the **seedling** is out, center it in the new pot. Gently add potting soil around it. Press the potting soil firmly around the base of the plant, then water it.

A Pot Prepared for Planting

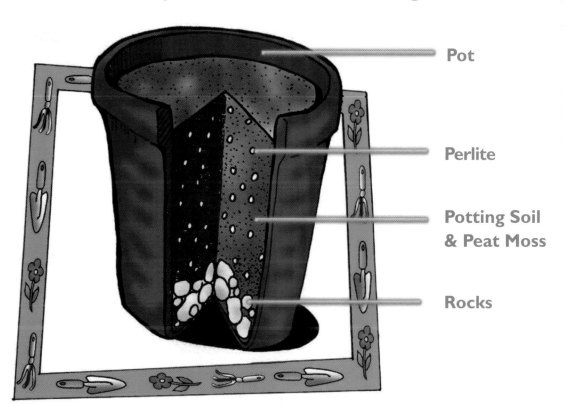

Pot

Perlite

Potting Soil & Peat Moss

Rocks

Propagation

Propagating a plant is a way to expand an indoor garden. Propagation is an easy and affordable way to create more plants. It can be done in many different ways. One method is to make stem cuttings.

To do a stem cutting, cut off part of a plant at the point where it meets the plant's main stem. Fill a cup with water and cover it with aluminum foil. Poke a hole in the foil, and stick the stem through the hole into the water. The foil will keep the stem from tipping over.

After the stem cutting grows roots, plant it in potting soil or a **rooting medium**. Make sure to keep the soil moist. Soon, your stem cutting will grow into a new plant!

Be gentle when you plant a stem cutting in soil, because roots that grow in water can be fragile.

The Right Spot

Once you've potted your plants, where should you put them? Some plants need lots of light. They would grow well on a sunny windowsill.

Other plants like **humidity**. They would thrive in a moist bathroom or kitchen. Whatever plants you've chosen, it's a good idea to keep them away from cold, drafty places.

What should you do if your home does not get much sunlight? You may want to try using grow lights. They are special lights that provide extra light for plants in homes with little natural light.

Grow lights can be set up anywhere in your home. Depending on the plant, the lights should be placed anywhere from 4 to 12 inches (10 to 30 cm) above the plant. The lights need to be shut off for about eight hours every night.

A bright, sunny windowsill is a great spot to start an indoor garden!

Terrariums

A special kind of indoor garden is called a terrarium. Terrariums are like tiny greenhouses. They are glass containers with **miniature** plants in them.

To make a terrarium, you will need a place to put your plants. An empty fish tank makes a good terrarium container. First, place a thin layer of coarse sand on the bottom. Then, add a layer of potting soil on top of the sand.

Next, plan how you want to arrange your plants in the terrarium. Start planting from the center and work your way out. Then use rocks, driftwood, ceramic animals, or birch bark to decorate around the plants.

Water the plants in your terrarium lightly, and only when the soil is dry. Set your new terrarium in medium light for one week. Then, move it into bright light after the shock of being **transplanted** has worn off the plants.

Terrariums are a fun way to garden indoors.

Greenhouses

A greenhouse is another place to create an indoor garden. A greenhouse's walls and ceiling are made from transparent material such as glass or plastic. This lets sunlight in and traps the warmth inside. Greenhouses are a good place to grow plants, especially in the cold winter months.

Greenhouses come in all different sizes and shapes. It's possible to visit a greenhouse at a garden center and see all the beautiful things that can be grown in one. Even the most **exotic** plants can survive through bitter cold winters in greenhouses.

If you don't have a greenhouse, but know somebody who does, ask him or her if you could have a small space for a few plants. Most gardeners are happy to share their space. Try growing ferns, flowers, or something else that you like.

Gardening in a greenhouse is a great way to make sure your plants get plenty of light and warmth, even in the cold winter months.

Caring for Your Garden

To care for your garden, you will need to give it water and **fertilizer**. Watering your plants is important. To see if your plant needs water, stick your finger about one inch (2.5 cm) into the soil. If the dirt is dry, you should water it. Water until the soil is evenly moist.

Plants should be fertilized in the spring and summer, or when they're blooming. Fertilizer contains **nutrients**, which help plants to grow.

Fertilizing a plant can be challenging. Not all plants need fertilizer. If you give a plant too much, you could burn the roots and kill the plant. So, be sure to check the care instructions that come with the **seedling** or seeds. Always have an adult help you apply fertilizer.

Some plants like moist soil. Other plants like to be watered only when their soil has completely dried out.

Pests & Problems

To keep your plants healthy, you will need to check them every day. If the plant is drooping, the lower leaves are turning yellow and falling off, and the soil is soggy, you may be watering too much. Let the soil dry out completely before watering again.

If your plants are growing long and spindly, and new growth is small and weak colored, the plant may need more light. Move the plant to a sunnier spot.

If you find bugs or spots on your plants, call a garden center. An expert will answer any questions you have about garden pests.

To prevent bug problems, clean your plants once a month. Wipe off their leaves, and pinch off any extreme growths.

Make sure to inspect your garden for pests.

An Indoor Project

Plants get their water from the soil. They draw it up through their roots and into their stems and leaves. You can watch this happen.

First, get a large glass and fill it with water. Next, add a few drops of food coloring to the water. Then,

cut one celery stalk from a bunch and put it in the water.

Soon you will be able to see the color of the celery stalk changing from the bottom of the stalk to the top leaves. You will see how plants drink water by watching the celery stalk turn colors!

A celery stalk will draw colored
water up to its leaves.

Indoor Plants to Try

What kind of plants can you grow? Cacti work well in an indoor garden. They need lots of light and little water. Cacti come in many shapes, colors, and textures. They also grow slowly, so you don't have to re-pot often.

Moss roses grow quickly with little care. They sprout fast from seeds, and produce brightly colored round blooms.

Most herbs also do well indoors. Rosemary, chives, thyme, and basil are easy to grow if you have a lot of sun. Fresh herbs from your garden taste great, too!

Ivies also grow well in an indoor garden. Ivies are especially fun because their long arms will wrap around anything they can reach.

Ivies don't have flowers, but their rich, green leaves have a nice shape.

Glossary

drainage - the process in which water runs off or dries up.

exotic - something new and different from far away.

fertilizer - a substance used to help plants grow.

germinate - to sprout and begin to grow.

humidity - moisture in the air.

miniature - a tiny version of something else.

nutrients - something naturally found in soil that helps plants grow.

peat moss - a pale green moss that grows in swamps and bogs.

rooting medium - a special soil mixture that provides a good environment for plants to take root.

seedling - a young plant grown from seed but not yet transplanted.

transplant - to move a plant from one spot to another.

Web Sites

My First Garden
http://www.urbanext.uiuc.edu/firstgarden/
This site is sponsored by the University of Illinois. This friendly site teaches visitors how to read a seed packet for important information. It also has sections on garden planning, tools, fertilizers, and more!

Field Museum: Underground Adventure
http://www.fmnh.org./ua/
This site is sponsored by the Illinois's Field Museum of Natural History. It teaches students about organisms that live in soil. Visitors can take a virtual tour of a terrarium. Another virtual tour introduces visitors to creepy, crawly critters and shows them what it's like to be a half inch tall!

These sites are subject to change. Go to your favorite
search engine and type in Indoor Gardens for more sites.

Index

B

bugs 24

C

conditions 16, 28
containers 8, 10, 12, 18

F

fertilizing 8, 22

G

garden journal 6
germination 10
greenhouses 4, 18, 20
grow lights 16

H

houseplants 4, 8

L

location 4, 16, 18

M

maintenance 22

N

nutrients 12, 22

P

planning 4, 6
plant life cycle 10
plant selection 4, 6, 28
planting 4, 10, 12, 13, 18
propagation 14

S

seedlings 8, 10, 12, 13, 22
seeds 8, 10, 22, 28
soil 8, 10, 12, 13, 14, 18, 22, 26
stem cutting 14
sunlight 10, 16, 18, 24, 28
supplies 4, 8, 10, 12, 14

T

terrariums 4, 6, 8, 18

W

watering 8, 13, 14, 18, 22, 24, 28